SAN FRANCISCO 49ERS SUPER BOWL CHAMPIONS

XVI, JANUARY 24, 1982
26-21 VERSUS CINCINNATI BENGALS

XIX, JANUARY 20, 1985
38-16 VERSUS MIAMI DOLPHINS

XXIII, JANUARY 22, 1989
20-16 VERSUS CINCINNATI BENGALS

XXIV, JANUARY 28, 1990
55-10 VERSUS DENVER BRONCOS

XXIX, JANUARY 29, 1995
49-26 VERSUS SAN DIEGO CHARGERS

SUPER BOWL CHAMPIONS

SAN FRANCISCO 49ERS

AARON FRISCH

CREATIVE PAPERBACKS

COVER: SAFETY RONNIE LOTT

PAGE 2: THE 49ERS DEFENSE CHASING DOWN A RUNNING BACK

RIGHT: QUARTERBACK JOE MONTANA LEADING THE OFFENSE

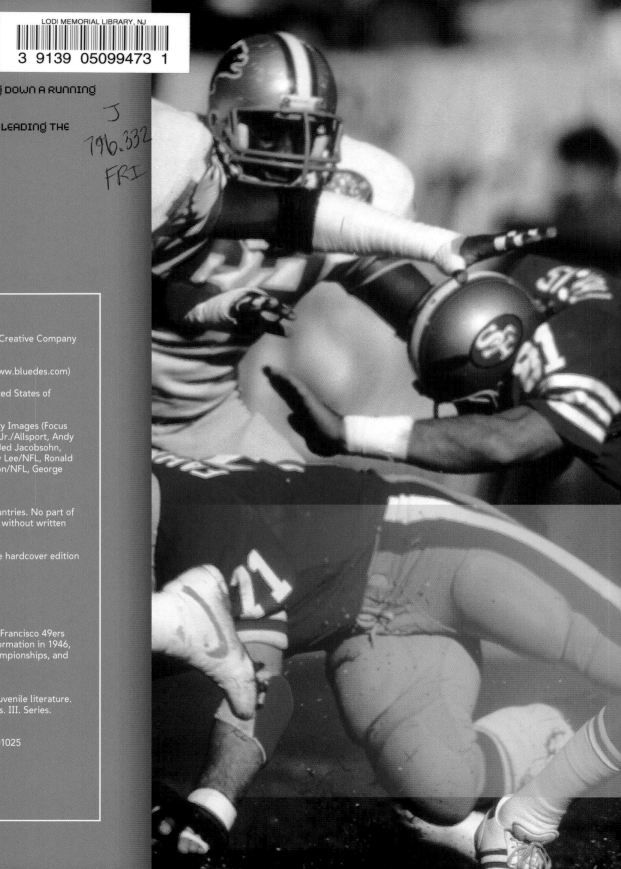

Published by Creative Paperbacks
P.O. Box 227, Mankato, Minnesota 56002
Creative Paperbacks is an imprint of The Creative Company
www.thecreativecompany.us

Book and cover design by Blue Design (www.bluedes.com)
Art direction by Rita Marshall
Printed by Corporate Graphics in the United States of America

Photographs by Dreamstime (Rosco), Getty Images (Focus On Sport, George Gojkovich, Otto Greule Jr./Allsport, Andy Hayt, Walter Iooss Jr./Sports Illustrated, Jed Jacobsohn, Heinz Kluetmeier/Sports Illustrated, Kirby Lee/NFL, Ronald Martinez/Allsport, MPS/NFL, Frank Rippon/NFL, George Rose, Travel Ink, Michael Zagaris)

The Library of Congress has cataloged the hardcover edition as follows:

Frisch, Aaron.
San Francisco 49ers / by Aaron Frisch.
p. cm. — (Super Bowl champions)
Includes index.
Summary: An elementary look at the San Francisco 49ers professional football team, including its formation in 1946, most memorable players, Super Bowl championships, and stars of today.
ISBN 978-1-60818-028-8 (hardcover)
ISBN 978-0-89812-592-4 (pbk)
1. San Francisco 49ers (Football team)—Juvenile literature.
I. Title. II. Title: San Francisco Forty-niners. III. Series.

GV956.S3F75 2011
796.332'640979461—dc22   2010001025

CPSIA: 012411 PO1420

9 8 7 6 5 4 3 2

CONTENTS

ABOUT SAN FRANCISCO... 7

49ERS FACTS... 8

UNIFORMS AND RIVALS... 9

49ERS HISTORY... 10

49ERS STARS... 16

WHY ARE THEY CALLED THE 49ERS?........................... 19

GLOSSARY.. 23

INDEX.. 24

SUPER BOWL CHAMPIONS

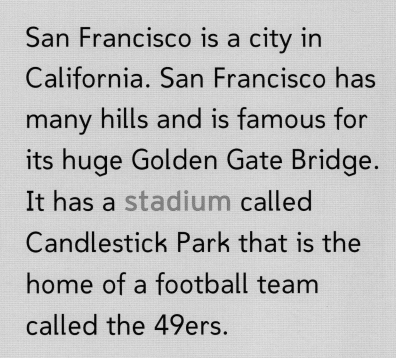

San Francisco is a city in California. San Francisco has many hills and is famous for its huge Golden Gate Bridge. It has a stadium called Candlestick Park that is the home of a football team called the 49ers.

... SAN FRANCISCO'S GOLDEN GATE BRIDGE IS MORE THAN A MILE LONG ...

49ERS FACTS

First season:
1946

Conference/division:
National Football Conference, West Division

Super Bowl championships:
XVI, January 24, 1982 / 26–21 versus Cincinnati Bengals
XIX, January 20, 1985 / 38–16 versus Miami Dolphins
XXIII, January 22, 1989 / 20–16 versus Cincinnati Bengals
XXIV, January 28, 1990 / 55–10 versus Denver Broncos
XXIX, January 29, 1995 / 49–26 versus San Diego Chargers

Training camp location:
Santa Clara, California

NFL Web site for kids:
http://nflrush.com

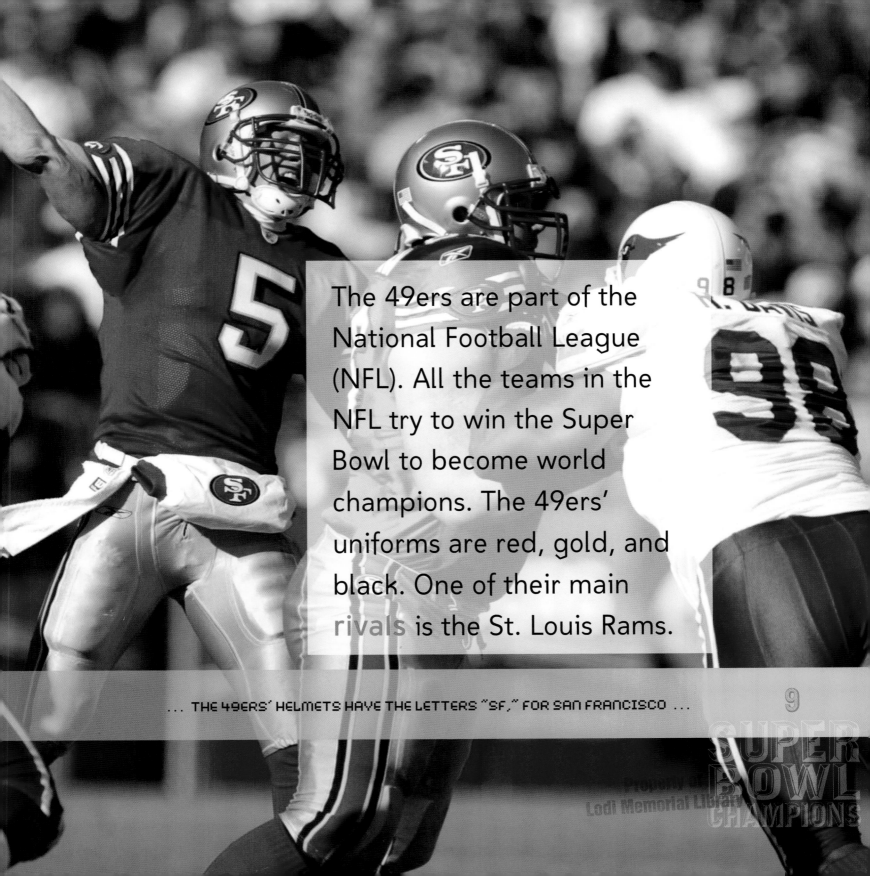

The 49ers are part of the
National Football League
(NFL). All the teams in the
NFL try to win the Super
Bowl to become world
champions. The 49ers'
uniforms are red, gold, and
black. One of their main
rivals is the St. Louis Rams.

... THE 49ERS' HELMETS HAVE THE LETTERS "SF," FOR SAN FRANCISCO ...

9

SUPER
BOWL
CHAMPIONS

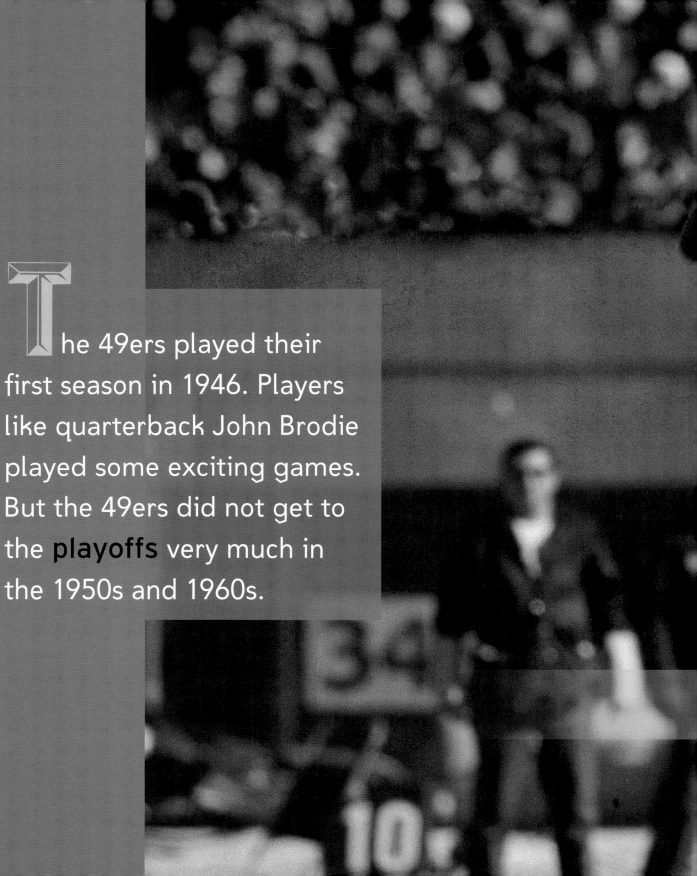

The 49ers played their first season in 1946. Players like quarterback John Brodie played some exciting games. But the 49ers did not get to the **playoffs** very much in the 1950s and 1960s.

... JOHN BRODIE PLAYED IN SAN FRANCISCO FOR 17 SEASONS ...

SUPER BOWL CHAMPIONS

SUPER BOWL CHAMPIONS

In 1978, the 49ers hired a new coach named Bill Walsh. The next year, they added **rookie** quarterback Joe Montana. The 49ers got to Super Bowl XVI (16) after the 1981 season. They beat the Cincinnati Bengals to win their first championship.

SUPER BOWL CHAMPIONS

... FANS CALLED STAR QUARTERBACK JOE MONTANA "JOE COOL" ...

13

The 49ers were the best team in the NFL in the 1980s. They won Super Bowls XIX (19), XXIII (23), and XXIV (24). Fans cheered as players like receiver Jerry Rice scored many touchdowns.

SUPER BOWL CHAMPIONS

Quarterback Steve Young led the 49ers to another championship. He threw six touchdown passes to help them win Super Bowl XXIX (29). The 49ers got to the playoffs six times after that.

... JERRY RICE (LEFT) AND STEVE YOUNG (RIGHT) ...

The 49ers have had many stars. Hugh McElhenny was a fast running back in the 1950s. Tight end Dwight Clark caught passes from Joe Montana. He made a famous catch in the 1981 playoffs.

... HUGH McELHENNY (LEFT) AND DWIGHT CLARK (RIGHT) ...

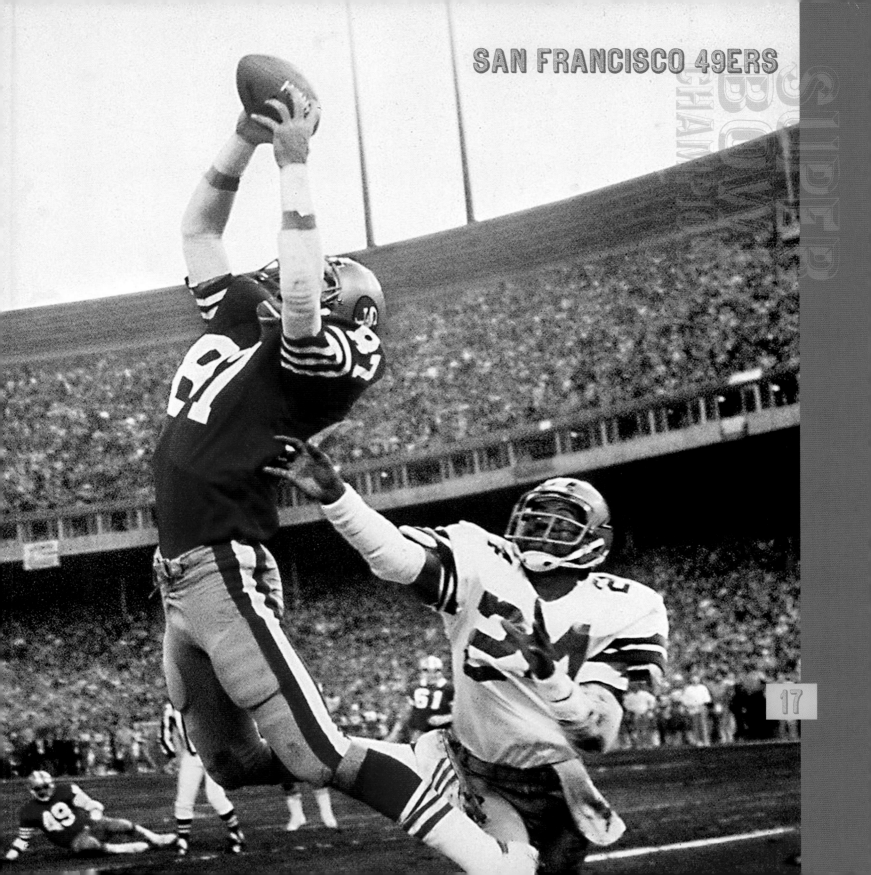

Roger Craig joined the 49ers in 1983. He was a tough running back who was hard to tackle. Ronnie Lott was another San Francisco star. He was a safety who hit hard and caused a lot of **fumbles**.

18

SUPER BOWL CHAMPIONS

WHY ARE THEY CALLED THE 49ERS?

In 1849, people found gold in California. Many people traveled there from all over the world hoping to find gold and get rich. Those people became known as "49ers."

... PATRICK WILLIS WAS SAN FRANCISCO'S LEADER ON DEFENSE ...

The 49ers added linebacker Patrick Willis in 2007. He made 137 tackles in his first season. San Francisco fans hoped that he would help lead the 49ers to their sixth Super Bowl championship!

21

SUPER BOWL CHAMPIONS

SUPER BOWL CHAMPIONS

GLOSSARY

fumbles — plays where the ballcarrier drops the ball on the ground before the play is over

playoffs — games that the best teams play after a season to see who the champion will be

rivals — teams that play extra hard against each other

rookie — a player in his first season

stadium — a large building that has a sports field and many seats for fans

SUPER BOWL CHAMPIONS

INDEX

Brodie, John 10–11

Candlestick Park 7

Clark, Dwight 16–17

Craig, Roger 18–19

Lott, Ronnie 18

McElhenny, Hugh 16

Montana, Joe 12–13, 16

playoffs 10, 15, 16

Rice, Jerry 14

Super Bowl . . . .
8, 9, 12, 14, 15, 21

team colors 9

team name 19

Walsh, Bill 12

Willis, Patrick 20–21

Young, Steve 15